THE LIFE & TIMES OF
LAWRENCE OF ARABIA

THE LIFE & TIMES OF

Lawrence of Arabia

BY
J. Anderson Black

SIENA

This is a Siena book
Siena is an imprint of Parragon Book Service Ltd

This edition first published by
Parragon Book Service Ltd in 1996

Parragon Book Service Ltd
Unit 13–17 Avonbridge Trading Estate
Atlantic Road, Avonmouth
Bristol BS11 9QD

Produced by Magpie Books Ltd, London

Illustrations courtesy of: Hulton Deutsch Collection;
Imperial War Museum, London; Mirror Syndication
International; Peter Newark's Pictures

ISBN 0 75251 576 4

A copy of the British Library Cataloguing in Publication
Data is available from the British Library.

Typeset by Whitelaw & Palmer Ltd, Glasgow

CHILDHOOD AND ADOLESCENCE

The life of T.E. Lawrence, the man who was 'Lawrence of Arabia', lies buried in sands of enigma. He died in 1935 in a motorbike accident, having long thrown over his romantic-hero fame for a life of barrack-room obscurity as an RAF mechanic. Even his friends hardly understood him, while the exasperated press dubbed him the 'Mystery Man'. Most secret of all were his origins, around which he drew a veil of steel, because they shamed him deeply. Yet it was his family, as much as the age in which he lived and his own genius, which made him Lawrence of Arabia – archaeologist, intelligence officer, warrior, statesman, writer, aircraftman and, above all, legend.

In the mid-1880s an Anglo-Irish squire, Thomas Robert Tighe Chapman, living in County Westmeath near Dublin, abandoned his family to live with the girl, Sarah, he had appointed governess to his four daughters. He also left behind him considerable wealth, for the Chapmans had counted for something in Westmeath since Elizabethan times, when they had been granted extensive lands, courtesy of a courtier cousin, Sir Walter Raleigh.

Embittered by her desertion, Chapman's wife

Edith, a severely religious woman known locally as the 'Vinegar Queen', refused a divorce. Although without prospect of a lawful union, the runaway couple proceeded to have five children, all boys. In their new life the couple assumed the name Lawrence, the surname the governess used (her real name is uncertain although it may have been Maden or Jenner, or possibly Junner – she was illegitimate) when practising her profession.

The Lawrences' transgression of the strict moral code of the Victorian age left them with a sense of guilt (in her dotage Mrs Lawrence was heard murmuring, 'God hates the sin but loves the sinner/God loves the sinner but hates the sin') and a fear of public exposure. For years they led an elusive, nomadic life, moving from Ireland to Wales, to Scotland, to Normandy, to England.

T. E. Lawrence in Arab dress

Thomas Edward Lawrence, the second of the sons, was born on 16 August 1888 at Tremadoc in North Wales, where the Lawrences had rented a small house, Gorphwyspha. The eldest of his siblings, Montague Robert (Bob), was born in 1885; William followed T.E. – who was known as Ned in the family – in 1889; Frank was born in 1893; and the youngest, Arnold, arrived in 1900. Even after settling in Oxford in 1896 – in order that their children could obtain a proper education – the parents were circumspect. Over-intimate social contacts were avoided, and there were few adult visitors to the family home at 2 Polstead Road, a semi-detached, solidly middle-class brick villa to the north of the city.

Those who did penetrate the portals of No. 2 found Mrs Lawrence a domineering woman, almost puritan in her attitudes. Unusually for a Victorian household, it was she who administered discipline, whipping the children on bare buttocks for misdemeanours. At the same time, she was also intensely loving and demanding. Lawrence came to resent his mother – his innately rebellious behaviour meant he was the most 'chastised' of the sons – but was also aware that he was the most like her. Physically, both were blond, with noticeably firm jaw lines and piercing blue eyes. But the similarities went beyond appearances. The determination and self-denial Lawrence would later show in the desert were also inheritances from his mother.

The father, meanwhile, was kindly and devoted to his sons. As was appropriate for a gentleman, even one in straitened circumstances, he did not work, and spent his leisure on bicycling and antiquarianism, both of which would become passions of T.E. himself. By the age of nine T.E. was already a zealous rubber of brasses, and had a secret arrangement to give Oxford workmen money in exchange for pieces of pottery they found when digging foundations. Summer holidays were spent bicycling around France, visiting, sketching and photographing castles (photography was also a passion, and many of the best images of his future desert war were taken by Lawrence himself).

If these were Lawrence's hobbies, there were less pleasurable demands on his time. The family attended St Aldates Church in Oxford three times each Sunday, and there were frequent Bible-readings at home. T.E. himself became a Sunday School teacher and a member of the Church Lads' Brigade. It was

Mrs Lawrence's hope that her sons might atone for her own failings by taking to evangelical Christianity. In this T.E. was a disappointment to her. As soon as he was able, he gave up churchgoing. Eventually he became an atheist.

Even in boyhood it was clear that T.E Lawrence was exceptional. He was precociously intellectual – his brother Bob later recalled that Ned could read the *Standard* newspaper upside down at the age of five – and had a marked liking for dangerous adventure. Famously, he navigated the underground Trill Mill Stream in Oxford in a punt, the first person to do so. And, as if to prepare himself for future rigours, he trained his body to accept little food and to endure physical hardship (at home he habitually slept in a wooden box). He was small in height –

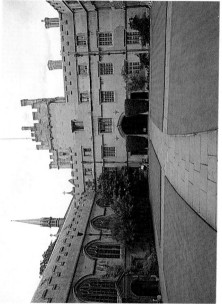

Jesus College, Oxford

five foot six when full grown – but immensely strong, 'a pocket Hercules', as he put it.

All five Lawrence brothers went to the Oxford City High School, a newly opened grammar school. T.E. did well academically, though not outstandingly, and later dismissed his schooldays as a waste of time. In particular he hated team games, and avoided them whenever possible. Some rigorous last-minute cramming enabled him to pass a scholarship examination to Oxford University, in January 1907.

At around the same time, Lawrence had discovered his illegitimacy, which provoked a personal crisis, causing him to leave home, bicycle to Cornwall and join the ranks of the Royal Artillery. After a few weeks he was bought out by his father. But the stigma of his bastardy would stay with him for ever.

Almost inevitably, given his interest in antiquarianism, Lawrence chose to read History at Oxford, officially joining Jesus College on 12 October 1907. According to University regulations he was to take up residence in college, but in fact continued to live at Polstead Road, where his parents built a small bungalow for him at the bottom of the garden. This shunning of normal college life gave him a reputation as an eccentric, which was reinforced by his unusual personal habits. Aside from his Spartan diet – which denied alcohol and smoking, as well as most foods – he tended to appear only at night, did little formal work, and spent much of his time reading medieval poetry and stories. (This courtly literature, with its chivalric codes and knightly heroes, had a profound effect on both his imagination and his later behaviour.) To the surprise, though, of his more literary friends, Lawrence was conformist enough to join the University Officers' Training Corps, where he proved an excellent marksman but exasperated the Company Sergeant-Major by his inability to wear a uniform smartly.

Lawrence's extracurricular interests left him badly prepared for his final examinations, and in consequence he was advised to submit a special thesis. He chose as his subject 'The influence of the Crusades on the medieval military architecture of Europe'. For this he decided to make a field expedition to Syria, alone and on foot.

At the bidding of a mentor, Dr D.G.

Lawrence and D. G. Hogarth in Cairo

Hogarth, the Keeper of the Ashmolean Museum in Oxford, Lawrence wrote for advice to the veteran Victorian explorer Charles Doughty, author of *Arabia Deserta*. Doughty was discouraging, suggesting that the hot climate and unfriendly inhabitants would make the trip hazardous. Lawrence was undaunted. He obtained, through the efforts of Lord Curzon, Chancellor of the University, an *irade* – a letter of safe conduct for Turkish-controlled areas of the Middle East – and bought a Mauser pistol. This proved a wise investment. At the end of his two and a half months in Syria in the summer of 1909, during which time he examined thirty-six castles and walked eleven hundred miles, he was attacked by a roadside robber, who was eventually driven off by a well-aimed shot.

When Lawrence returned to Oxford his family hardly recognized him. He was emaciated by malaria and lack of food. But the desert had fascinated him, especially its vastness and silence. To keep out the sound of 'civilized' Oxford, he draped the walls of his garden bungalow with rugs. Meanwhile, the knowledge of Crusader fortifications he had gleaned during his Syrian sojourn earned him, in the summer of 1910, a First Class Honours Degree.

ARCHAEOLOGIST

In only a matter of months Lawrence was back in the desert. After graduating, he secured, through Hogarth's influence, a postgraduate scholarship at Magdalen College, which came with an annual income of £100; more importantly, Hogarth offered Lawrence a place on the excavation he was undertaking for the British Museum of the great Hittite mound at Carchemish in Syria, on the banks of the Euphrates.

Lawrence arrived at the site in March 1911, and would spend most of the next three years there, his particular responsibilities being the photographic record of the dig and the organization of the workforce. This virtual exile suited him. He became fluent in Arabic, and took to dressing like an Arab. He also became great friends with the Arab workmen, especially the site foreman, Sheikh Hamoudi, and a fifteen-year-old boy, Dahoum, who lived with him as a companion. The latter arrangement gave rise to speculation on the site that Lawrence was homosexual – especially when he had Dahoum pose for a nude sculpture which he then exhibited on the roof of his quarters – but it was almost certainly a desire to shock which made him so careless of social convention. Lawrence, in fact, was asexual; he had no interest in sex. The harsh desert, however, continued to captivate him. He wrote home: 'Here one learns the economy of beauty. England is fat – obese.'

By 1913 the golden years at Carchemish were drawing to a close. The Kurds of Northern Syria, restless under Ottoman rule, planned to attack the town of Aleppo, where the British Consulate was defenceless. Lawrence, along with Leonard Woolley, who had taken over as excavation director from Hogarth, helped smuggle guns through to it. In Europe, meanwhile, it seemed that a war between Britain and Germany was becoming inevitable. A clash with Germany's ally, the Ottoman (Turkish) Empire, which controlled much of the Middle East, would naturally follow.

Consequently, the British Foreign Office

thought it prudent to monitor Turko-German activities in the region, and recruited some unofficial spies to do so. Lawrence was soon on the books, keeping a particular eye on the building of the Berlin–Baghdad Railway, which was financed and supervised by the Germans. In turn, Lawrence recruited Sheikh Hamoudi and Dahoum as intelligence gatherers, even taking them to Oxford in July 1913 for training.

Then, at the end of 1913, Field Marshal Lord Kitchener, the British Agent in Egypt, organized a geographical survey of Turkish-controlled Western Sinai. To give a plausible cover to what was essentially a military reconnaissance, the survey was conducted under the auspices of a respectable archaeological organization – the Palestine Exploration Fund. Woolley and Lawrence were asked to join the expedition, which was headed by Captain S.F. Newcombe of the Royal Engineers.

The party spent six weeks covering the Sinai Desert, surveying tracks and waterpoints, with Woolley and Lawrence gathering material on the area's archaeology. The archaeologists and the professional soldier got on well, despite rations austere enough to test even Lawrence's taste: the daily menu was bread and Turkish Delight, for all meals.

The expedition proved a success, although the Turks eventually realized they had been duped. To ease the tension Kitchener urged that Lawrence and Woolley publish their official archaeological record. They returned to England in June 1914 for its writing, *The Wilderness of Zin* duly emerging in December.

But by then there was no need to appease the Turks. The world was at war, and Britain and Turkey on opposite sides. And T.E. Lawrence was to find his destiny.

INTELLIGENCE OFFICER

For Britain, the First World War started on 4 August 1914. On hearing of its outbreak, Lawrence wished to get into uniform as quickly as possible, a sentiment shared by a whole generation of Englishmen. It was natural, given his pre-war spying activities, that he should be directed towards espionage work and in September he found himself in London, being interviewed by Colonel Coote Hedley, head of MO4 (Military Operations 4), the geographical division of

Lawrence in army uniform

Military Intelligence. Hedley already knew of Lawrence and took him on immediately, despite Lawrence's casual manner and dress. Lawrence received his commission as a second lieutenant a month later, being put on the 'special list', a War Office category for personnel with no official regiment. His first duty was to produce a map of the area he had just travelled over, Sinai.

In mid-October Lawrence wrote to his brother Will, then teaching in India but already fired with the patriotism that would take him to a death on the Western Front: 'I am going out to Egypt probably, at the end of this week, on special service. The Turks may do something in that direction . . .' On 4 November after some hesitation, Turkey joined the war on the side of Germany and her allies. In December, Lawrence joined the intelligence staff at General Headquarters in Cairo.

The British Army in Egypt was desperate for Arabic-speaking officers; Lawrence was an obvious choice. So were his erstwhile colleagues Woolley and Newcombe, both of whom joined him in Cairo, where they helped set up an intelligence unit, attached to the General Staff, under the command of Colonel Gilbert Clayton. As in London, Lawrence served as a map officer, but his duties soon involved the interrogation of newly captured Turkish prisoners of war and the recruitment of spies. In time, he would be transferred early in 1916 to the Foreign Office's intelligence branch in Cairo, the famed Arab Bureau, where he edited its intelligence summary, the *Arab Bulletin*, and served as the Bureau's link with Military Intelligence.

Clayton, Lawrence's superior officer at both GHQ and, later, the Arab Bureau, quickly came to respect his subordinate's talents and was prepared to overlook his quirks – which were considerable, particularly in a junior officer. One colleague recalled Lawrence in Cairo as being 'an extremely youthful insignificant figure, with well-ruffled light hair, solitary pip on sleeve, minus belt and with peaked cap askew.' Never one to take pomp or authority easily, Lawrence routinely 'forgot' to salute.

If his job as an intelligence officer was valuable, it was still desk-bound. Lawrence was fighting the war with a map-case; increasingly he wanted to fight it with a gun. As 1915 progressed his dissatisfaction became greater, not least because the year claimed the lives of his brothers Frank and Will, in May

and October respectively, in the maelstrom of
the fighting on the Western Front. 'They
were both younger than I', he wrote to his
Oxford friend E.T. Leeds, 'and it doesn't
seem right, somehow, that I should go on
living peacefully in Cairo.' Lawrence's peace,
in fact, was soon to end.

In March 1916 Lawrence, now a captain,
along with a colleague, the aristocratic adven-
turer and MP Aubrey Herbert, was sent on a
field mission to the broiling, fly-blown plains
of Mesopotamia (now part of Iraq), where a
British military force was in trouble. Des-
patched from India, the force had reached
almost to the outskirts of Baghdad, where it
had been driven back by crack Turkish troops,
and was now besieged and starving in the small
town of Kut-el-Amara, on the River Tigris.

The purpose of Lawrence's mission was unusual; he was to bribe the Turks into giving up the siege. He was authorized to spend up to £1 million on this purpose.

By the time Lawrence, Herbert and Colonel Beach, the overall head of the mission, reached Mesopotamia, their journey was in vain. There was no longer any possibility of the British buying their way out of Kut-el-Amara; the Turks would accept nothing but unconditional surrender. Lawrence's task, instead, became one of getting the best surrender terms. After overtures, the Turks let 1000 wounded British go in return for 1000 able-bodied Turkish POWs. Of the remaining 9000 British soldiers, most died on a forced march to Turkey.

The tragedy of Kut appalled Lawrence. On

the long return trip to Egypt he wrote a scathing report, which found every aspect of the campaign wanting, from its basic concept to the standard of the maps used. The report had to be toned down before it could be shown to the Commander-in-Chief in Egypt, General Sir Archibald Murray. Lawrence, meanwhile, arrived back in Cairo in June 1916, the month of the Arab Revolt.

WARRIOR

The Revolt of Grand Sherif Hussein and his sons against Ottoman rule, the moment and the movement which would give Lawrence his great opportunity, had been some considerable time in the making. Most of the Arab peoples had been under Turkish rule since the sixteenth century. Throughout this long period, the Arabs had shown little inclination to unrest. In 1908, however, a new regime in Turkey had begun to insist on the Turkification of the Ottoman Empire.

The result was an upsurge of Arab nationalism, and the formation of Arab parties dedicated to the formation of an independent Arab state.

Foremost among the Arab nationalists was Hussein Ibn Ali, the aged Grand Sherif of Mecca, a descendant of the Prophet Muhammad, and ruler of the province of Hejaz, which bordered the Red Sea. With Turkey embroiled in the world war, Hussein saw his chance. On 10 June 1916 he took the shot which, literally, opened the insurrection, firing a rifle round from his Mecca balcony at the neighbouring Turkish barracks. Britain, of course, was only too delighted to help an enemy of Turkey; the problem lay in finding a practical way to do so. The British did not want to commit troops it desperately needed on the Western Front, and the Arabs – being

Muslim – were anyway not keen to have large numbers of infidel Christians in their lands.

In the event, Britain dispatched some old artillery pieces and rifles, and, as a morale booster, issued a set of commemorative stamps of the Sherif. (These were actually designed by Lawrence in Cairo, who sent a set home for his youngest brother, Arnold. The stamps had flavoured gum, 'so one may lick without unpleasantness'.) Soon, the revolt began to lose momentum. In October 1916, therefore, Ronald Storrs, the Oriental Secretary at the British Agency in Egypt, was sent to the Hejaz to confer with the Arabs about the revolt's progress. Lawrence, already filled with enthusiasm for the Arab cause, asked for, and was granted, permission to go with him. This was the chance Lawrence had been waiting for. He wrote later in *Seven Pillars of Wisdom*, his epic work on the Arab war: 'I had believed these misfortunes of the revolt to be due mainly to faulty leadership, or rather the lack of leadership, Arab and English. So I went down to Arabia to see and consider its great men.'

In Jedda, on the Red Sea, Lawrence and Storrs met with the Emir Abdulla, one of the aged Sherif's sons, all of whom acted as his commanders in the field. Afterwards, Storrs returned to Cairo, while Lawrence journeyed to see Hussein's other sons. The eldest of them, Ali, Lawrence thought 'nervous and tired'; the youngest, Zeid, immature. On 23 October Lawrence arrived in the camp of Hussein's third son, Feisal. 'I felt at first glance', he records in *Seven Pillars*, 'that this was the man I had come to Arabia to seek –

the leader who would bring the Arab revolt to full glory.' Feisal, Lawrence found, was vigorous, clever and imposing. He was further impressed by the toughness of Feisal's camel-riding tribal warriors ('seldom were men harder'), although he also believed that their individualism and inexperience might prove problematic. Lawrence rushed back to Cairo, where his argument that Feisal should be considered the pre-eminent Arab commander quickly gained acceptance. So did his suggestion that instead of troops, Britain should send advisers to help Feisal. He was taken at his word. Within days, he was sent back to the Hejaz, which would become his theatre of operations for the next two years. Lawrence of Oxford, of Carchemish, of Cairo, was now Lawrence of Arabia.

When Lawrence arrived back in the Hejaz as liaison officer to Feisal at the beginning of December 1916, the situation was near disastrous. A surprise advance by the Turks had panicked part of Feisal's army, the fear spreading to a force under the command of his youngest brother, Zeid, whose men had ridden in wild retreat to the Red Sea port of Yenbo. Under a further attack from the Turks, Feisal himself – who, to Lawrence's relief, remained cool amidst the madness – was obliged to fall back on Yenbo as well. The situation was saved by three ships of the Royal Navy, which took up stations in the harbour, where their guns and searchlights could command the route of any Turkish advance. The Turks attempted to assault the town at night but, met with a menacing silence and a wall of brilliant beams from the searchlights on the ships, became convinced they were facing a superior force and withdrew. That night, Lawrence believed, 'the Turks lost the war'.

Yenbo proved to the Arab forces that the Turks were not invincible. Keen to exploit the victory, Lawrence urged Feisal to attack another port, Wejh, 180 miles to the north. This involved the movement of Feisal's entire army of 8000 men, of numerous parochial – and often rival – tribes, across a barren and waterless wasteland. The march to Wejh in January 1917 was a triumph of organization for the Arab guerrillas, their sense of accomplishment on arrival only slightly dimmed by the discovery that Wejh had already been taken by the Royal Navy and a small force of Arabs led by a British Army lieutenant, Charles Vickery. There had been many casualties among the attacking force,

and Lawrence was angry because he believed
that they could have been avoided. 'To me,'
he wrote in *Seven Pillars*, 'an unnecessary
action, or shot, or casualty, was not only
waste but sin . . . Our rebels were not
materials, like soldiers, but friends of ours . . .'
Lawrence would always feel the loss of
human life, even among the enemy, strongly.
As he saw it, if Vickery and the Navy had
waited for Feisal's army, the town could have
been surrounded and would surely have
surrendered. This would not be the last time
that Lawrence would clash with more
conventional army officers, many of whom
thought him 'bumptious'. More, they loathed
his adoption of Arab dress, which they saw as
affectation but which he found a practical
necessity ('army uniform was abominable
when camel-riding'), and which in any case
he had become used to at Carchemish. A gift

from Feisal of a magnificent white-silk, gold-embroidered kaftan was a particular item of dislike.

Although Wejh was an irritation to Lawrence, it was also an important victory for the Arab Revolt, and opened up the possibility of an even more desirable objective 100 miles further up the coast – the port of Akaba, which Lawrence had last visited during the Sinai-mapping expedition. If Akaba could be taken, it would not only bring more territory into the revolt, it would directly threaten the Turkish lifeline in the desert, the Hejaz Railway, the southernmost end of a line that ran from Turkish-held Damascus to Medina.

The capture of Akaba, which came about on 6 July 1917, was a shining success. Not only

General Allenby

did Lawrence plan it, but he also led the
operation, journeying deep into the desert
hinterland with Sherif Nasir of Medina and
the veteran Howeitat chief, Auda Abu Tayi,
to raise support. Alone, Lawrence undertook
deep-reconnaissance mission to the gates of
Damascus, before rejoining Nasir and Auda.
Their 2000-strong force then swept down to
Akaba, annihilating a Turkish battalion in a
skirmish at Abu el Lissan (in which Lawrence,
in the excitement of the moment, shot his
camel through the head). Lawrence and the
Arabs raced the last few miles to the port
through a driving sandstorm and splashed into
the sea. The Turkish garrison, stunned by the
direction of the attack, from the north-east,
which they had thought was almost
impossible, hardly loosed off a shot.

The capture of Akaba changed, at a stroke,

Abdullah, Allenby and Lawrence at a
military review

the whole complexion of the war in the Middle East, allowing the desert campaign under Feisal – with Lawrence as his adviser – to be fought in close relation to the main British thrust against the Turks, under the new C-in-C, General Sir Edmund Allenby. Not long after Akaba was taken, 'The Bull', as Allenby was nicknamed, called Lawrence in for an interview at his HQ in Cairo. The General was not quite sure what to make of the small bare-footed man before him. Lawrence asked for additional weapons and £200,000 in gold. After a moment's thought, Allenby replied, 'Well, I will do for you what I can'. He also gave Lawrence a free hand to fight the desert war as he wished.

So Lawrence returned to the Hejaz with Allenby's blessing, and a decoration for his role at Akaba (a Companionship of the Bath, for which he had to be promoted to major), and began a guerrilla war against the Turks, targeting in particular their railway. Using an old fort at the desert oasis of Azrak, he sallied forth to blow up track and trains, and cause as much disruption to Turkish rail traffic as possible. Although Lawrence did not invent this activity, he soon became a past master at it (it is noteworthy that the British Army issued *Seven Pillars of Wisdom* to Resistance leaders during the Second World War as a 'how-to' guide). His bravery and physical strength awed his Arab companions, and also those British soldiers who occasionally accompanied him. To the astonishment of Sergeant W.H. Brook, his Stokes machine-gunner, the slight Lawrence could out-shoot and out-ride the Arabs and 'seemed immune to the fiercest heat'.

But the guerrilla 'stunts' began to take their toll on Lawrence's body and mind. By late September 1917 he was writing to a friend in Oxford: '. . . nerves and temper going . . . This killing and killing of Turks is horrible.'

His 'nerves and temper' were frayed further when he was captured and homosexually raped in the town of Deraa, south of Damascus, on 20 November 1917.

Lawrence had decided to make a reconnaissance of this Turkish stronghold, accompanied by a peasant guide. As they walked through the town, Lawrence, in disguise, was stopped by a Turkish sentry and recognised (Lawrence was already infamous amongst the Turks). According to his later account in *Seven Pillars*, he was then taken before the Bey (the Turkish Governor), who tried to rape

him. When rejected by Lawrence, the Bey
turned him over to his guards, who took turns
to whip him and rape him. (To a friend,
however, after the war, Lawrence confided
that in fact the Bey had also sodomized him.)
Somehow, Lawrence managed to escape
before dawn, and fled the town, eventually
rejoining his own men. But the assault at
Deraa left him with physical and mental scars
which would never heal.

There were other cares as 1917 drew to a
close. Lawrence began to be plagued by guilt,
believing that the Arabs were fighting on the
strength of an assurance of post-war self-
government which the Allies – and especially
Britain and France, the two powers jostling
for influence in the region – would ultimately
betray. As the representative of Britain
Lawrence was forced to dissemble to his Arab

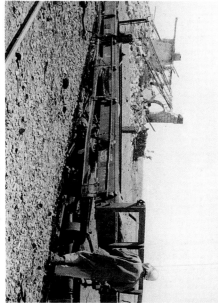

Train-wrecking on the Hejaz railway

friends, who trusted him implicitly. The more Lawrence's influence grew, so did he sense of shame.

The war in the Hejaz desert, meanwhile, was becoming more and more orthodox. Akaba had been heavily reinforced, with men and material pouring into the port. For reconnaissance Lawrence was no longer reliant on the camel; he also had the choice, of aircraft, armoured cars, or specially adapted Rolls-Royce, as well as British troops to man them.

Late in January 1918 there occurred the only conventional battle of Lawrence's career, at Tafileh, about 100 miles north-east of Akaba. This remote mountain village had been taken with ease on the 15th by 300 Arabs led by

Auda, whose loud cry to the Turkish defenders 'Dogs, do you not know Auda?', had been enough to break the Turks' resolve. Ten days later, however, the Turks launched a 1000-strong frontal attack on Tafileh, in a snowstorm, but the Arabs – under Lawrence's tactical guidance – repulsed them. The Turks lost 400; the Arabs 25. The official British history of the war termed it 'a brilliant feat of arms'. For his part, Lawrence was awaded the DSO to add to his unworn collection of decorations, and promoted lieutenant-colonel.

By now, Lawrence was finding the strain of war near intolerable. His body so dreaded further pain and privation from disease, wounds, cold and hunger that he had to force himself to go into combat. He asked to be relieved of his post, but there was to be no

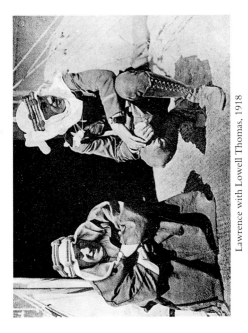

Lawrence with Lowell Thomas, 1918

escape. He was too important. So he went back to train-wrecking, bridge-blowing and raids on Turkish installations. The days dragged by, Feisal's forces operating as quick-raiding guerrilla's on the flank of Allenby's northward drive through what was then Palestine. And then suddenly the war was rushing towards its end – though it still had one great act for Lawrence: the capture of Damascus.

Throughout the summer of 1918 the Turks had been falling back everywhere, and Allenby decided to deal them a mortal blow. On 19 September he began an advance on Damascus, the historic capital of the Arabs. This drive north and eastwards, known as the Battle of Megiddo, proved to Allenby's greatest victory – by 25 September the Turkish forces had been driven back over

the Jordan, retiring on Amman and then
Damascus. Simultaneously, a mobile Arab
column under the command of Feisal and
Lawrence was to seize and take Deraa – the
town of his humiliation – which was the
major railway station south of Damascus.
Accompanying Lawrence was a young
officer of the Royal Engineers, Lieutenant
Alex Kirkbride, who left a vivid account of
Lawrence the destroyer. 'Knowing his habit
of using unnecessarily large amounts of
explosives,' Kirkbride wrote in his memoir
An Awakening, 'I asked him to give me
plenty of notice so that . . . I could get my
men away to safety before he blew up the
bridge.' Lawrence's reply was a dismissive
'Oh, all right, all right, don't fuss!' Almost
immediately, Kirkbride continued, 'there
was a terrific detonation and an arc of bridge
flew high into the air and fell all around my

people.' Lawrence almost fell over laughing. Later that evening, he made a conciliatory gesture by inviting Kirkbride to coffee. Surrounding Lawrence was his bodyguard, a small private army, up to 90 strong, recruited from the most reckless Ageyli, or tribeless, Arabs. In this last phase of the war the Turks had placed a high price on his head.

After Deraa had been isolated and the Turks had pulled back, Lawrence decided to march on Damascus himself. At Tafas on 27 September he caught up with the troops of a Turkish rearguard who, in an act of spite, had butchered the village's inhabitants. The Arab force following on – which included the local Sheikh, Tallal – became wild with rage, and flung themselves on the Turks, showing no mercy. Lawrence himself gave the order, the

Disguise worn by Lawrence in enemy territory

first and last time he would do so in the war, to take no prisoners.

In time Lawrence would become revolted by his bloodthirstiness at Tafas, but in the heat and excitement of late September 1918 he pressed on towards Damascus with scarcely a backwards glance. He had become consumed by a grand idea. He intended to get to the city before the other Allied forces and claim it for the Arabs, establishing Feisal as the head of an independent Arab regime in Syria. At a stroke Lawrence would expiate his own guilt at what he saw as his betrayal of Arab aspirations, and free the Arabs, whose cause he had come to love.

But by 30 September troops of General Sir Henry Chauvel's Australian Mounted Division had already entered the outskirts of

T. E. Lawrence by James McBey, 1918, Damascus.
Imperial War Museum, London

Damascus, and all other Allied units had been ordered to halt. Seeing his chance disappearing, Lawrence jumped into 'Blue Mist', his Rolls-Royce car, and sped towards the city. Lieutenant Kirkbride saw him rush past: 'I waved, but Lawrence did not look around; he was staring ahead in the same fixed way I had noticed a few days before [as he rode out of Tafas].'

Just outside Damascus, Lawrence met Sherif Nasir of Medina, Feisal's cousin, and sent him into the city to raise the flag of the Hejaz Revolt. This, however, had already been done by two Algerian brothers, Mohammed Said, who had declared himself Civil Governor, and Abd el-Kadir, both of whom Lawrence disliked (he suspected Said of being a pro-Turksih spy and, indeed, of having betrayed him in Deraa). When he entered the

city on 1 October, 'Lurens' removed the
Algerians and installed Shukri el-Ayubi, a
local pro-Hussein nationalist, as Governor.
By now Damascus was in an euphoria of
liberation and a chaos of looting and political
intrigue. To bring the situation under control
'we called out the Arab troop,' wrote
Lawrence in his official report, 'and put
Hotchkiss [machine guns] round the central
square, and imposed peace in three hours,
after inflicting about twenty casualties.'

On 3 October General Allenby and Emir
Feisal each arrived in the city. The two
principals were introduced at the Victoria
Hotel, with Lawrence in attendance. The
meeting was historic but unhappy. Allenby
dramatically told Feisal that under the Sykes-
Picot Agreement of 16 May 1916, whereby
Britain and France agreed to the division of

the Ottoman Empire between them after the eventual peace settlement, France was to be the protecting power in Syria. Feisal was to have the administration of Syria, but only under French guidance. Moreover, Allenby continued, the Arabs were deemed to have no claim to the Lebanon or Palestine, the former going to France and the latter to Britain.

The Arabs, after all, were not free. Lawrence had failed in his mission. Dismayed, he asked Allenby if he could take the leave owed to him. He left Damascus for England that night.

Feisal

STATESMAN

Lawrence arrived back in England on 24 October 1918. Eighteen days later the Armistice was signed and the Great War was over. But not, for Lawrence, the cause of Arab liberation. Over the next three years he tried to secure in the council chamber what he had failed to win by force of arms.

Just five days after landing he appeared before the august Eastern Committee of the British War Cabinet. Reporting on the situation in

Arabia, he proposed his own political solution, which gave high place to the sons of Hussein. The minutes of the Committee noted: Colonel Lawrence's own idea was the establishment of Abdulla as ruler of Baghdad and Lower Mesopotamia, Zeid in a similar position in Upper Mesopotamia, with Feisal in Syria.'

Next day, 30 October, Lawrence had an audience with the King, officially to be invested with the CB and DSO. Having arrived at Buckingham Palace, however, he politely informed the King that he could not accept the honours because His Majesty's Government had broken pledges to Feisal which Lawrence had given in the King's name. The King later recalled, 'There I was holding the box in my hand'.

Meanwhile, there had arisen the problem of who should speak for the Arabs at the Peace Conference which was shortly to take place in Paris, in which the 'Allied and associated powers' were to determine the settlement of the treaties with Germany, Austria–Hungary, Turkey and Bulgaria. The intermediary assigned to the Arab question was Colonel T.E. Lawrence, who cabled Sherif Hussein: 'I trust you will send Feisal, as he has gained a personal reputation in Europe through his splendid victories . . .'

And so, on 6 February 1919, Feisal, accompanied by Lawrence, made his case for an independent Arab state in Syria to the main body of the Peace Conference, the Council of Ten, which consisted of the leaders of the ten main Allied governments. What followed added much to Lawrence's growing lustre. Lawrence read out an English translation of Feisal's speech to the Council, at which President Wilson of the USA asked him if he would also read the speech in French, since several members only understood that language. Lawrence did so flawlessly. The Ten, for a moment, forgot their great stature, and clapped like enthusiastic schoolchildren. It was perhaps small surprise that many at the Peace Conference thought Lawrence, wearing Arab headdress with his British Amy uniform to underline his commitment to Feisal, its most intriguing figure.

Yet, despite Lawrence's personal charisma, the Ten failed – largely because of French objections – to install Feisal as King of Syria. Lawrence, depressed, returned to Oxford, where he spent day after day sitting alone in his room, hardly moving.

These days of despair drew out into months, and then years. To the bitterness of personal defeat were added other problems. His father had died of influenza in April 1919, Lawrence arriving from Paris too late to see him alive. He was injured in an air crash in May, while flying to Cairo, suffering a broken collarbone, broken ribs and mild concussion. (Not that this put him off flying, which was to have a significant influence on his later life.) He also began writing his account of the war in Arabia, often working on it for hours at a stretch without food or sleep. For a title, he used that of a pre-war novel he had started to write but then thrown away: *Seven Pillars of Wisdom*.

And then there was his fame, perhaps the biggest strain of all, although his attitude to it was ambivalent.

ST NICHOLAS

JULY, 1927

THE WHITE KING of the ARABS
by Lowell Thomas

Illustration to a Lowell Thomas article
on Lawrence

It was almost overnight that Lawrence became the most romantic, most famous hero of the First World War. During the war knowledge of his exploits had been confined to military and establishment circles, but this was remedied in 1919 by an American film-maker, Lowell Thomas, who had first met Lawrence in Jerusalem in 1918. With the war's end, Lowell devised an 'illustrated travelogue' about the campaign in the Middle East called originally '*With Allenby in Palestine*, but so successful was the section on Lawrence's part in the campaign that *'and Lawrence in Arabia'* was tacked on to the title. The show played first in New York in March of 1919, and then transferred to London, where it was booked for two weeks at Covent Garden from 14 August. It ran, instead, for six months, moving in 1920 to the Royal Albert Hall and then the Queen's Hall. Afterwards, it toured the world for four years, making Lawrence an international celebrity.

According to Thomas, Lawrence went to see the show in London several times, although if spotted he would blush and rush away. In an apt phrase, Thomas said of Lawrence: 'He had a genius for backing into the limelight.'

Eventually, Lawrence would decide to stay out of the limelight altogether, but there remained one more public duty.

In July 1920, the French bombarded Damascus and drove Feisal (newly crowned King of Syria) and his Provisional Government from the country; in Mesopotamia (Iraq) in June, the British ruthlessly suppressed Arab 'rebels' at a cost of

Feisal and Lawrence at the peace conference, 1919

many lives – British as well as Arab – and £50 million. Such instability and expense prompted the British Colonial Secretary, Winston Churchill, to try a new settlement for the area. He offered Lawrence an advisory post, who gladly accepted. The salary was £1200 per annum – which Lawrence, surviving only on a small income from a Fellowship of All Souls College, Oxford, desperately needed – but more importantly he had another chance to right the wrongs done to the Arabs.

So in March 1921 Lawrence returned to the Middle East, as a senior adviser to Churchill at the Cairo Conference. The new settlement – much of it Lawrence's handiwork – put Feisal on the throne of Iraq and made his brother Abdulla Emir of Trans-Jordan. Compared with the 1919 settlement after the Paris Peace

Conference, this was a distinct improvement for the Hussein dynasty. Lawrence believed he, and Britain, had finally fulfilled the wartime obligations to the Arabs, and he would look back on his part in the agreement as his greatest work. The settlement endured more or less intact until the 1950s, and the Hussein dynasty still rules in Jordan.

Lawrence wanted to give up his job with the Colonial Office as soon as the Cairo Conference was concluded, but Churchill persuaded him to stay on until July 1922. On 4 July Lawrence officially tendered his resignation. Less than two months later, to the consternation of his friends, he enlisted in the Royal Air Force under the alias 'John Hume Ross', Aircraftman 2nd Class, No 352087.

AIRCRAFTMAN AND WRITER

Lawrence's experiences in the RAF are recorded in his book *The Mint*. Life in the ranks imposed a great physical strain on him – at thirty-four he was considerably older than most of his fellow recruits, and still suffered from assorted wounds – and he found training a torture. It did, however, give him mental respite. As he himself noted, the armed services were the modern form of the monastery. He wanted a rest from fame and inner turmoils and responsibility. The RAF, as he put it, gave him the chance of a 'brain sleep'.

Unfortunately, the 'brain sleep' did not last long. After training, A/C2 Ross was posted to the Farnborough School of Photography in early November 1922. Five weeks later he was recognized. The story was splashed over the front page of the *Daily Express* on 27 December under the headlines 'UNCROWNED KING AS PRIVATE SOLDIER/FAMOUS WAR HERO BECOMES A PRIVATE/SEEKING PEACE'.

Shortly afterwards Lawrence was discharged from the Air Force, which, like the other services, deeply disliked and mistrusted almost all forms of publicity.

Clouds Hill

Determined to continue with his life in uniform, he joined the army. Once again he changed his name, this time by deed-poll, and so Aircraftman Ross became No. 7875698 Trooper Shaw, T.E. of the Royal Tank Corps. He chose the surname Shaw because it was that of two of his friends, the famous dramatist George Bernard Shaw and his wife Charlotte, who had virtually adopted him as their son.

Trooper Shaw was posted to the Royal Tank Corps Depot at Bovington, Dorset, on 12 March 1923. He disliked the peacetime army, finding its ranks full of society's rejects. Almost inevitably, his fellow soldiers guessed who he was – he was different from them in his age, his class and his education – but gradually accepted him as 'Broughie' Shaw, the nickname deriving from the admired

Brough Superior motorbike he rode for recreation, usually at top speed, around the nearby narrow lanes.

He was still writing and rewriting *Seven Pillars of Wisdom*, an enterprise which proved impossible in barrack Hut 12. He searched for a retreat where he might work undisturbed. One mile north of Bovington Camp was Clouds Hill, a derelict cottage, which he was able to rent for a small sum. Apart from his parents' house at Polstead Road, Oxford, it became Lawrence's only real home, and he was to keep it on until his death. There he received friends from the camp, as well as such literary acquaintances as the novelist E.M. Forster.

Another visitor to Clouds Hill, however, went for distinctly non-artistic purposes. This was John Bruce, a Scotsman, who had joined the Tank Corps at the same time as Lawrence, and apparently at his instigation. At Clouds Hill Bruce was paid by Lawrence to administer a series of ritual floggings. Lawrence, like the medieval saints he had read about as an undergraduate, believed that sex dissipated the vital forces of the body and that by flogging he could purge his soul of carnal desire.

There were other desires in Lawrence, too. Although he had come to accept army life he was obsessed with rejoining the Air Force. All his requests were turned down. In 1925 he went as far as to hint at suicide. This threat, and the influence of his friends John Buchan, Bernard Shaw and Sir Hugh Trenchard, Chief of the Air Staff, led Prime Minister

Stanley Baldwin to issue a directive that Lawrence be allowed to re-enlist in the RAF. Trooper Shaw was transferred to the RAF on 18 August 1925, and posted to the Cadet College at Cranwell. There he was contented, working as a clerk and occasionally as a mechanic. He loved aircraft, and would sneak into hangars to wash them down out of sheer enjoyment.

It was at Cranwell that he finally finished his Herculean labour on *Seven Pillars of Wisdom*. He had not only written every page but, in keeping with a long-standing interest in the craft, had designed it to reflect the peak of the art of making books. Every page, where possible, had its own illuminated initial letter, and the text was liberally accompanied by drawings by his favourite artist, William Roberts. The book was dedicated to 'S.A.', assumed to be Selim Ahmed, alias Dahoum, the boy he had befriended at Carchemish over a decade before.

A popular abridged version of *Seven Pillars*, entitled *Revolt in the Desert*, was published in 1927. Fearing that publication would whip up another press frenzy about him, Lawrence asked to be posted for service abroad. In December 1926 he sailed for India.

Lawrence was in India for nearly two years. Initially he was stationed at Karachi, but senior officers disliked his presence on camp and so he was transferred to the fort at Miranshah in Waziristan, on the Afghan border. While there he translated most of Homer's *Odyssey* for an American publisher. Another activity to which he devoted much free time, not always gladly, was writing

Aircraftman T. E. Shaw in India

letters – hundreds of them – to friends, and sometimes to the strangers who inquired after him.

This Indian exile was brought to an end by the sort of sensation he had tried to avoid. A tribal revolt in Afghanistan coupled with the close presence of ex-Colonel Lawrence, suitably incognito, proved too much of a temptation for Fleet Street. There were days of headlines and stories alleging that 'the arch-spy of the world' was behind the unrest, seeking to thwart Russian ambitions in Afghanistan and is neighbour states. The government of India decided that Lawrence should be returned to England, and Trenchard concurred. The 'arch-spy' sailed home in January 1927 aboard the mail liner SS *Rajputana*.

Arriving at Plymouth on 2 February, Lawrence was whisked away to his new posting at RAF Mount Batten. The waiting media, though, managed to get some blurred photographs and film footage of 'Lawrence of Arabia'. In only a few years' time they would use these images to adorn his obituary.

LEGEND

Mount Batten was one of Lawrence's happiest postings. The commanding officer, Wing Commander Sydney Smith, was benevolent and gave Lawrence the freedom of his home. The work was to Lawrence's liking, too. In the summer of 1929 he assisted Smith in the RAF team which managed the Schneider Trophy seaplane races. Mostly, though, he was employed as a mechanic (ever since childhood, he had demonstrated an unusual mechanical ability), tuning and testing experimental craft for the RAF's Marine Equipment Branch.

During the course of this work, on 4 February 1931, he witnessed a fatal air crash in Plymouth Sound, when a flying-boat nose-dived into the sea. Along with Smith, Lawrence rushed to the scene in a tender and six out of twelve airmen were saved. Lawrence, though, was convinced that more could have been saved if a faster boat had been available. This became a personal crusade and he worked on high-speed rescue boats until February 1935. As in Arabia, he proved himself a brilliant amateur. The boats went on to save many lives in the Second World War.

In February 1935 Lawrence was cast adrift

from the RAF. He was forty-six and sadly aware of ageing (for the first time in his adult life he no longer looked boyish). Outside of an old dream of setting up a printing press, Lawrence had little idea what to do. Many of his friends hoped he would take up a post equal to his ability. Informally, he was offered the Secretaryship of the Bank of England, and the task of organizing Britain's Defence Forces. He turned both down. The author Henry Williamson, meanwhile, wanted to recruit him to the British Fascist Movement.

Always interested to meet a fellow writer, Lawrence decided to invite Williamson for lunch at his cottage. Lawrence left Clouds Hill in the morning on Monday 13 May 1935 and motorbiked into Bovington, from where he sent Williamson a brief telegram:

Lawrence after leaving the RAF

'LUNCH TUESDAY WET FINE.
COTTAGE 1 MILE NORTH OF
BOVINGTON CAMP.'

Returning on his Brough to Clouds Hill,
Lawrence swerved to avoid two errand boys
on bicycles. The motorbike went out of
control, Lawrence was thrown over the
handlebars, hit the ground hard and fractured
his skull. He was taken, in a coma, to the
hospital at Bovington camp, where he died
without regaining consciousness six days later.
He was forty six.

A figure of mystery in life, it was inevitable
that, in death, T.E. Lawrence should become
the subject of speculation. For years after
there were rumours of assassination and
conspiracy. It is much more likely that
Lawrence, who once said he would try to

avoid hitting a chicken in the road, would have taken any action to avoid the two boys (one of whom was slightly injured). And possibly, the gloom of leaving his beloved RAF meant his mind was not on the road. The inquest, hastily convened for the morning of 21 May, the same day as the funeral, returned a verdict of accidental death.

Lawrence of Arabia was buried, following his wishes, in the annexe to the graveyard of St Nicholas's Church, Moreton, not far from Clouds Hill. The coffin was carried by six pallbearers representing the various stages of his life. There were tributes from all over the world, and from all ranks of society.

Predictably, the only nation not to mourn his death was Turkey, where newspapers trumpeted the death of 'an infamous spy' who had once been the 'King of the Desert'.